JAAZ Nspiration

On Sunday Morning

The Collection

A Message from the Teacher

Jacqueline Marie Norris, M.A.Ed

JAAZ Nspiration

On Sunday Morning
The Collection

A Message from the Teacher

Jacqueline Marie Norris, M.A.Ed

Published by:

Jaaz Creative Designs

Copyright © 2021 by Jacqueline Marie Norris
San Francisco, California

Jacqueline Marie Norris, M.A.Ed, asserts the moral right to be identified as the author of this book.

All rights reserved. No part of this publication may be reproduced, distributed, or transmitted in any form or by any means, including photocopying, recording, or other electronic or mechanical methods, without the prior written permission of the publisher, except in the case of brief quotations embodied in critical reviews and certain other noncommercial uses permitted by copyright law. For permission requests, write to the publisher, addressed "Attention: Permissions Coordinator," at the address below.

Jaaz Creative Designs
PO BOX 347217
San Francisco, CA 94134
jaazworld@gmail.com

Cover Design Concept: Jacqueline Marie Norris
Content Editor: Rikki Lynn Norris
Editor: Leesha Langlois

Praying Hands art work designed by Maurice Jacquel Maxwell

Book Concept Inspired by:
Sis. Rosie Lee Atkins & Sis. Mildred Bailey

Jaaz Nspiration Supporters:
Evergreen Baptist Church, San Francisco, CA
JN Notary & Professional Services
JN Outreach Foundation, Inc.
JAAZWORLD.COM
Fatt Sak Records

Written and Printed within the United States of America

ISBN-13: 978-0-9998703-3-4

On Sunday Morning Message Finder

Preface vii
Introduction ix
Prayer xi
Seeking Confidence...*Rev. Bobby Brown* 1
Don't Look Back ... *Rev. Jackey Wilson* 3
When You Find God, You Find Life... *Sis Lecia Wilson* 5
Making Wise Choices ... *Sis. Jacqueline Norris* 8
Using Our Words Wisely ...*Sis. LaTasha Knighten* 10
We Need Each Other ... *Rev. Abraham Gunter* 13
Speak the Truth Boldly ... *Rev. Bobby Brown* 19
Am I Dealing with What I Am Feeling? ... *Sis. Jacqueline Norris* 20
Priorities ... *Sis. Lecia Wilson* 23
A Healing Touch ... *Rev. Bobby Brown* 26
What Is in Your Heart... *Sis Lecia Wilson* 28
Be Aware of Anger & Malice... *Sis. Jacqueline Norris* 31
Empty Rituals are Useless... *Rev. Bobby Brown* 34
Are You Comfortable in Sin? ... *Sis. LaTasha Knighten* 36
Do You Have a Relationship With God?... *Rev. Jackey Wilson*.. 39
Conclusion 41
History 42
Special Thanks 47
Puzzle 48
Author Bio 49

PREFACE

I was introduced to Evergreen Baptist Church at an early age. Evergreen was founded in 1945 by the late Rev. Ruth Johnson. From what I am told it started with a small Sunday School class in his home on Ingalls Ave, San Francisco. One day God led him to build a church between two mountains, 6270 Third Street in San Francisco, CA.

While I am not sure when my grandmother, Rosie Lee Atkins, joined but it was way before 1971 which is when I was born. For as long as I can remember I was connected to the hip of Sis. Rosie Lee Atkins when it came to church attendance. She was my role model when I did not even now know what that meant. She was more than a grandmother, she was a caregiver, a wife, a mother, a business woman, a loyal friend, strong willed, beautiful, classy, and her food was amazing! Rosie Lee (aka Big Momma) wore many hats at the church. I fondly remember her being a teacher and member of the Pastor's aide. As a child I would love to play in her Sunday shoes. At the time I had no idea that I would literally be walking in those same shinny pointy-toed high-heel shoes.

She was stern and she provided way too much structure, or so I thought. Today I value every sacrifice she made while raising me the best that she could. She instilled so many values and so much foundation it is over flowing. I no longer take the values and foundation she provided for granted. I now do my best to offer those some principals to others rather they are in church or not. Sunday morning was a big deal in our house on Carr Street. It actually started on Saturday night. Back then, we had to *prepare for church we did not roll out of bed and look for an outfit on that morning, everything was a plan. It was the time that we prepared our outer temple to receive the goodness of the Lord for our inner temple, the dwelling place of the Lord.*

Today, I teach Sunday School as my grandmother did and like she, I love it! "On Sunday Morning", is a collection of words that you can hear from spiritual teachers of Evergreen Baptist Church.

INTRODUCTION

Ephesians 4:11 – 16 is the foundation scripture for this book. [1] And he gave some, apostles; and some, prophets; and some, evangelists; and some, pastors and teachers; [12] For the perfecting of the saints, for the work of the ministry, for the edifying of the body of Christ: [13] Till we all come in the unity of the faith, and of the knowledge of the Son of God, unto a perfect man, unto the measure of the stature of the fulness of Christ: [14] That we henceforth be no more children, tossed to and fro, and carried about with every wind of doctrine, by the sleight of men, and cunning craftiness, whereby they lie in wait to deceive; [15] But speaking the truth in love, may grow up into him in all things, which is the head, even Christ: [16] From whom the whole body fitly joined together and compacted by that which every joint supplieth, according to the effectual working in the measure of every part, maketh increase of the body unto the edifying of itself in love.

Teachers of the Word are critical to the learning, edifying, and growing process of a Christian. Evergreen Baptist Church has been blessed to have an abundance of good teachers. While this book only high-lights snippets from six teachers, evangelist, missionaries, ministers, and pastors who have spoken God's word on a Sunday Morning, please know that there are and were so many more. Currently many people find themselves struggling with their relationship with God and the Church. I have found that some people have a hard time separating the two. In any case, the words of a Spirit filled Teacher can sooth the soul, encourage, strengthen, express love, and provide clarity in the times of confusion. (Titus 2:7-8; 1 Peter 4:10; Deuteronomy 32:2; and 2 Timothy 2:15)

I pray that something within "On Sunday Morning – The Collection" reminds you or encourages you to continue to seek the face of the Lord daily (1 Chronicles 16:11).

PRAYER

May God bless you as you delve into the messages. May you receive the words within the pages as encouragement, strength, and love. To fully embrace each message, we recommend that you say a simple pray prior to reading then let the Word touch, heal, and reveal.

In Jesus name, we pray. Amen.

In the space below feel free to document anything that is or has been holding you back from living the life that God has for you. As you read *"On Sunday Morning"* begin to release those strongholds and find complete comfort in the word found in Psalms 107:13-14 "Then they cried to the Lord in their trouble, and he saved them from their distress. He brought them out of darkness, the utter darkness, and broke away their chains."

Psalm 34:17

The righteous cry out, and the LORD hears them, he delivers them from all their troubles.

Let the Church Say Amen!

SEEKING CONFIDENCE

By Rev. Bobby Brown
Romans 10: 5-17

───────────

Salvation comes to all who confess Jesus Christ as Lord and believe in their hearts. As Christians, we believe the message of the gospel applies to all who will hear, believe, and obey it. Part of our Christian duty is to joyfully serve or support mission causes committed to spreading the gospel. We should use God's word as we are led by the Holy Spirit, especially when proclaiming the good news of Jesus. God's word should be evident in what we say and what we do. Trusting God from the depths of one's being and making a sound, bold confession leads to a righteous standing with God.

Paul used this thought to reinforce the point that God's true desires is that all who genuinely seek him would receive the blessing he has to give. Anyone who calls on the name of the Lord shall be saved. God will never disappoint anyone who trusts him by neglecting to impart his righteousness after they have believed in him. We can neither control nor be responsible for someone else's choice to receive or reject Christ. With a focus on faith and salvation, this message should challenge us to trust. God is in every aspect of our spiritual walk. Salvation is available to everyone, but people receive the good news only when others care enough to share it. You will never reach the lost without a serious understanding that everyone you know desperately needs to be saved (your family, friends, co-workers, neighbors, and strangers).

What are you willing to do to draw others to Christ? God used someone to draw you closer to him. This week identify and seek someone who may be lost or drifting in his/her spiritual commitment. Share your story and the good news of Jesus Christ. Embrace with joy at the possibility of salvation for all.

Amen.

DON'T LOOK BACK

By Rev. Jackey Wilson

God is good!

We have come this far by faith, no matter what trials or tribulations we have experienced in the past; God continues to grant us new mercies and an abundance of blessings. Don't look back and don't be discourage because of the past, God has a blessing in store for you. In Genesis 19:17 the angel told Lot's his wife and his daughters to leave the city and not to look back. The angel was giving them a warning. God was upset due to all of the sin that was going on in Sodom and Gomorrah and he had decided to destroy the city. As the story goes on we find that Lot's wife disobeyed the angel and looked back and unfortunately she turned into a pillar of salt. The morale of the story is when God speaks or gives you an assignment, it would be wise for you to proceed on the path that he prepares and don't look back. We as Christians must learn to leave what is in the past in the past. God has already forgiven us so there is no need for us to relive the past. It is impossible to fix or re-due our past but we can ask God to forgive us and let him direct us through our future.

As 2021 comes to a close, step out on faith, let God lead you and let's not look back. You will be tempted to look back or to bring the past into your future but just remember God is always available to you. Our God is a good God he will never fail. His

Mercy and goodness will endure forever. Trust in the Lord and be prepared to receive all that he has in store for you.

God Bless and remember, "Don't Look Back".

Amen.

WHEN YOU FIND GOD, YOU FIND LIFE
By Sis. Lecia Wilson

What does it mean to find God? To truly find God in the biblical perspective, we must acknowledge His Presence, seek Him, follow Him, change our attitude for the better, and attain spiritual growth. It can also be an adjective for people who have transformed their lives for the better or have cleansed themselves from vices and other worldly things. Acknowledging God's presence in our lives is finding God. By acknowledging His presence, we are also seeking His presence. Presence in Hebrew means face. So, to seek God's presence, it means to seek God's face, literally. For modern-day Christians, it means to seek God's presence in our everyday lives. Scripture tells us that God is everywhere, but it is through Jesus Christ that we can communicate with the Father and the belief that He is the Way, the Truth, and the Life. By doing this, we are acknowledging the presence of God in our lives.

<u>John 14:1-6</u> Let not your heart be troubled; you believe in God, believe also in Me. In My Father's house are many mansions; if it were not so, I would have told you. I go to prepare a place for you. And if I go and prepare a place for you, I will come again and receive you to Myself; that where I am, there you may be also. And where I go you know, and the way you know. Thomas said to Him, "Lord, we do not know where You are going, and how can we know the way?

Jesus said to him, I am the way, the truth, and the life. No one comes to the Father except through Me.

Finding God Means to Follow Him. To find God means to follow Jesus Christ and His teachings as written in scripture. Following Him means surrendering your heart and mind to Him. It also means receiving the grace of faith through Him as written in the Bible. Following Him also means asking for forgiveness for our sins. Human as we are, we have trespassed, and it is our duty to ask forgiveness for all our sins in order to follow Jesus and find God.

<u>Ephesians 2:8-10</u> For by grace you have been saved through faith, and that not of yourselves; it is the gift of God, not of works, lest anyone should boast. For we are His workmanship, created in Christ Jesus for good works, which God prepared beforehand that we should walk in them.

Finding God means a Change of Attitude for the Better. Finding God also means changing ourselves for the better. This does not mean merely changing our physical attributes or worldly values. Rather, it is emphasized in the Bible that in order to find God, it is important that we improve ourselves spiritually. It is important that we change our perspective of God and life in general to a better outlook.

If you make it your practice to give a little attention to every thought of God you have, you will soon start believing each thought of God is God. This is how believing works. Believing, at least in the way Jesus expressed it, has little to do with content and everything to do with conduct. This is how faith grows and believing, or trusting works. So, as you make your new way of thinking a habit yet you feel that God cannot be found; do not worry God is in us already waiting for us to take action. As you make this your daily practice, soon it will become your way of daily living.

<u>I Corinthians 3:16</u> Do you not know that you are the temple of God and that the Spirit of God dwells in you?

When you actually realize this, then you have found GOD!

Amen.

MAKING WISE CHOICES
By Sis. Jacqueline Norris

This topic covers a wide variety of issues such as trust, honor, belief, faith, and historic choices. I know that sound like a lot but each one connects to the next. In Joshua Chapter 5 and 6 we are made aware that Joshua was the next chosen leader by God's hand and HIS divine appointment. He was tasked with taking the people to the promised land. Keep in mind leading them to the promise land was not just about getting to the other side. It was mostly about their free will decision to follow God, trusting the unknown, and realizing that everything promised by God is obtainable. The catch to that statement is, **IF** they obey. That in itself is a practical lesson that can be applied to our everyday lives. While the story of Joshua took place long ago the concept and process remain relevant today. The battle at Jericho was won without a physical fight.

What situation have you faced or are dealing with where you have or are seeking to use physical resources instead of spiritual resources? Well, by reading the following scriptures you will see that God has a plan for you that can lead to victory without you exercising physical strength. You will be called to apply trust in God, listen to HIS instructions, be obedient, and last but not least you will see the benefit of giving God all the glory.

Have you built a wall around your heart, home, or your family? A wall where no one can get in or out? Are you attempting to shield yourself and those you love from physical, mental, or worldly harm? Side note: Nothing you can do or build can protect you or your family like the Lord. Instead of spending your energy on that, invest more time in prayer and watch God do amazing things for you as well as those you love. Trust GOD

Reference Scriptures: Proverbs 3:5-6, Psalm 37:4-5, Psalm 33:20-522, Isiah 26:34, Psalm 56:3-4, and Jeremiah 17:7-8.

Imagine how Joshua may have felt as he stood there glaring at the huge wall and having full knowledge of standard military strategy. His physical eye and mind showed him the impossible and he may have felt hopeless yet his trust and love for God superseded his fleshly feelings. As he obeyed God's exact instructions the wall came down. Was it magic? No, it was a result of trust, obedience, belief, and the ability to move self out of the way and allow God to step in with ALL power.

Final Thought: Trust in the Lord with all your heart and lean not on your own understanding; in all your ways submit to him and he will make your path straight. Proverbs 3:5-6

Amen.

USING OUR WORDS WISELY

By Sis. LaTasha Marie Knighten

As kids many of us played a game where when someone said something mean to us, we would say, "sticks and stones may break my bones but words may never hurt me". Today we will turn our focus on the following statement: "Sticks and stones may break my bones, but words can kill my spirit".

As Christians we must be careful how we speak to one another. We must catch ourselves before we start a fire. Sometimes you might feel it is necessary to start the fire because you might feel that the person deserves a fire; however, we have to remember that God is the one who decides what we do and do not deserve. You can think of it this way, how would you feel if God decided to unleash a fire on you? That in itself would cause many of is to immediately change our course, thinking, and behavior.

Our tongues are the deadliest weapons we have and the majority of the time it is often uncontrolled as a result of our frustration. We can tame our tongues by starting with our heart. Remember, you don't have to say everything that you think. Many times, your face expressions tell people what you are thinking. The following scriptures will help you gain self-control of your tongue.

Proverbs 21:23 Whoever guards his mouth and his tongue keeps his soul from troubles.

Proverbs 10:31 The mouth of the righteous bring forth wisdom, but the perverse tongue will be cut off.

Proverbs 16: 23-24 The heart of the wise teaches his mouth and asked learning to his lips. Pleasant words are like honeycombs sweetness to the soul and healthy to the bones.

Proverbs 18:21 Death and life are in the power of the tongue and those who love it will eat its fruits.

You may be asking, what does all that mean?

In summary, we have to watch our mouths as well as how we say what we say. While I understand that that task can be very difficult; we have to remember that our words have a definite impact and affect others. The Word of God is not tailored for our expectations. His word is tailored for his expectations for us. When we say that we love God that indicates that we are willing to follow God's way.

Using our words wisely has the power to direct others and help them see the benefit of giving their life to Christ and joining His eternal kingdom of heaven. There are so many people who are holding onto the earthliness or negative words and unfortunately many do not know that it is causing them to stumble or may be causing them not to live freely in Jesus Christ. For many of us the negative words that have been spoken to us or that we heard when we were younger are still with us today as adults. When we use our words to communicate with others, we are planting seeds; that includes negative words and/or positive words. Therefore, we all should realize that the type of verbal seeds we are planting will grow and will need pruning or replanting. Be careful about the seeds that you are planting into others as it has the power to give life or kill the spirit

As a side note, choosing your words wisely does not mean that you should not tell the truth or shy away from certain conversations. As Christians it is mandatory that we tell the truth, while doing so, the delivery is key. Imagine the postman walking up to your house and throwing all of your mail at you rather that delivering it to your hand or putting it in your mailbox. It was about the delivery! The delivery of the truth is normally what upsets us or causes us to be off balance. If the postman put the mail directly in the mail box or hands it to you nicely both parties would find common ground or satisfaction by doing something the correct way. On the other hand, when the mail is thrown, it becomes scattered and we instantly become angry, frustrated, and for some uncomfortable. The communication at that point is lost and so is the opportunity to display Christ like behavior.

It is very important for us to demonstrate Christ like behaviors when we talk to one another especially our children or the youth. We should think about our words and actions and remember that there is a time to be firm nurturing as well as a time to be compassionate and gentle. The key is to ask God for directions, and allowing Him to direct us on what to say and what not to say to others.

Let us remember that our words have the power to give life. Pray and do your best every day to seek God's direction when communicating with His people!

Amen.

WE NEED EACH OTHER

Sermon by Rev. Abraham Gunter

———————

"But Scripture has locked up everything under the control of sin, so that what was promised, being given through faith in Jesus Christ, might be given to those who believe. Before the coming of this faith, we were held in custody under the law, locked up until the faith that was to come would be revealed. So the law was our guardian until Christ came that we might be justified by faith. Now that this faith has come, we are no longer under a guardian. So in Christ Jesus you are all children of God through faith, for all of you who were baptized into Christ have clothed yourselves with Christ. There is neither Jew nor Gentile, neither slave nor free, nor is there male and female, for you are all one in Christ Jesus. If you belong to Christ, then you are Abraham's seed, and heirs according to the promise." **Galatians 3:22-29**

Our scripture today shows us that in order to receive the promise as descendants of Abraham, we were in custody under the law until Christ came. And now through faith, believing in Jesus Christ, we have been set free from the penalty of sin.

We are now justified by faith!

To recap, In Christian theology, justification is God's righteous act of removing the condemnation, guilt, and penalty of sin, by grace, while, at the same time, declaring the unrighteous to be righteous, through faith in Christ's atoning sacrifice.

Faith is not knowing what lies ahead, but trusting and believing in the One who created the past, the present, and the future! Faith in God changes our perspective on how we view things. Faith puts our trust in God and not in self. Faith is trusting that God is faithful whether or not he does what we want Him to do.

Faith is knowing with certainty that our destination is planned by God. And having the certainty that we will reach our destination.

My message is to let you know that, I need you and you need me!

Therefore, accept one another, just as Christ also accepted us, for the glory of God." Romans 15:7

We demonstrate our acceptance of each other, through service, through prayer, and through love. We serve each other when we apply God's Word to our lives.

"Do nothing out of selfish ambition or vain conceit. Rather, in humility value others above yourselves, not looking to your own interests but each of you to the interests of the others. In your relationships with one another, have the same mindset as Christ Jesus: Who, being in very nature God, did not consider equality with God something to be used to his own advantage; rather, he made himself nothing by taking the very nature of a servant, being made in human likeness." Philippians 2:3-7 NIV

What shall I do to help my brother or sister? If I can help somebody as I pass this way, then my living shall not be in vain!

We must accept others, the good and the bad attributes they may have, by praying for them. Only God can change the hearts and disposition of our neighbor. The Bible says pray for those who despitefully use you. Prayer is the key and faith unlocks the door. Prayer changes things.

I need you and you need me.

God created us so we would have a relationship with each other. He first created Adam, and then He created Eve which created the first relationship. This relationship produced a family, which has led to generations of families. Even in the most beautiful situation such as family love, sin crept in.

Adam and Eve were manipulated and persuaded to defy God's plan for them. Then they tried to hide from God in the Garden of Eden. Another example, Cain became jealous of Abel and killed his brother which led him to become separated from his family.

Why is there such a need to separate ourselves from each other?

Today we separate ourselves because of status, gender, culture, race, denomination, commonalities, and by political party etc. Let me remind you that God has not called us to be separated, because we are one in Christ Jesus! We who believe in Jesus Christ as Savior and Lord, are of the seed of Abraham, and are connected in the Body of Christ. The body of Christ cannot have separate entities. We must come together and show the world what unity looks like within the people of God.

Our origin, all starts with that first family. In Christ we are one, descendants of Abraham because of our faith and belief in Christ Jesus.

What is our common goal?

A common goal causes people to pull in the same direction.

It is amazing how people working toward the same goal, are able to put aside their differences in order to complete a task! We as Christians have been given a task of developing relationships with each other. A task that will not get done until we without reservation, apply the Word of God each day to our walk!

I need you and you need me!

By this all people will know that you are my disciples, if you have love for one another."

I believe our goal as Christians should be to adhere to what Matthew 22:37-40 says: "Jesus replied: Love the Lord your God with all your heart and with all your soul and with all your mind.' This is the first and greatest commandment. And the second is like it: 'Love your neighbor as yourself. All the Law and the Prophets hang on these two commandments."

Our primary goal should be to show the love of Christ to all, who we come in contact with. I say this because in 1Corinthians 13, scripture tells us of three virtues that work together to demonstrate Christian beliefs: they are Faith, Hope, and Love it reminds us that the greatest of these is Love.

We know we are saved by grace through Faith which means we can weather any storm, because our Hope is in Christ Jesus.

So why is love so important?

When I was growing up, we were required to say a verse before we ate dinner. Our dad would bless the food, and then my two sisters and I, had to say a verse, before we could start eating. Well, I always wanted to say mine first. It would be short and sweet. It was either Jesus Wept, or God is love. Love is important, because God is love, and He tells us that the two greatest commandments, involve loving Him, and loving each other. I've learned that anything I do or say that does not have some form of love attached to it, is not of God. 1Corinthians 13:4-8 says: "Love is patient, love is kind. It does not envy, it does not boast, it is not proud. It does not dishonor others, it is not self-seeking, it is not easily angered, it keeps no record of wrongs. Love does not delight in evil but rejoices with the truth. It always protects, always trusts, always hopes, always perseveres and Love never fails.

Love is patient- it is not proud or self-seeking. When in a relationship everything does not always have to go your way. Patience because of my love for my neighbor, allows me be still and let God work things out. When we are waiting for someone to change, it may not happen as fast as we want it to happen. We must be patient, and wait on the Lord. He hears and he will answer our prayers in His time according to His will.

Love keeps no record of wrongs- love will not allow you to bring up the past to win an argument. When we learn to keep no record of wrongs there will be no need to forgive. We at times refuse to forgive, because we are still holding someone accountable for the past mistakes they've made. Forgiveness is a choice! Choose to let go of the past and keep moving forward in your relationships.

Love does not delight in evil but rejoices with the truth- desiring payback is evil. Vengeance is mine says the Lord.

We are here to make a difference in this world! I believe that we sometimes fail in our witness for Christ because we do not let love guide us. We tend to pick and choose who we will share the Gospel of Jesus Christ. As the body of Christ, let us put aside our differences and come together united, demonstrating to our neighbor, what it means to be saved, to be a Christian, to be a child of God.

God's Word says: If you confess with your mouth that Jesus, is Lord. Don't be ashamed to tell your neighbor about the God you serve and believe in your Heart that God raised his Son from the grave and thou will be saved. In 2 Chronicles 7:14 God gives us a common goal: "If my people, who are called by my name, will humble themselves and pray and seek my face and turn from their wicked ways, then I will hear from heaven, and I will forgive their sin and will heal their land."

I need you and you need me!

Our land and the people around us will be healed and delivered when we decide to do what we were placed here to do. We are here to show the love of Christ to everyone we meet. To lift up the name of Jesus and to be a witness for Christ and to praise, glorify, and honor Him in Spirit and in Truth. The voice of the church must be heard but not separated, we must be unified in our message of love. We can accomplish so much more when we work together, than we can when we work separately.

Our relationships should not be based on our differences, but on our obedience to our Lord and Savior, who has made us all sisters and brothers in the Body of Christ!

Amen.

SPEAK THE TRUTH BOLDLY

By Rev. Bobby Brown
1 Kings 22:15-23, 26-28
Romans 1:28-32

Since the beginning of time, God's formula for life with him remains unchanged; obey and live, disobey and die. God's word is set before us daily. We must choose whether to receive and obey it. Those who are spiritually blind choose to disregard the word of God to their own disadvantage. God speaks to and through those who know him and his word and enables them to stand boldly by the power of the Holy Spirit. God is calling for those who will refuse to compromise and be "yes-men" when it comes to his word and his mission in the world.

Today's church is constantly challenged to remain true to what the Lord has said: God expects every believer to have the courage to speak the truth. We live in a time when people would rather go along to get along rather than risk being persecuted, criticized, and ostracized for speaking the truth.

This message challenges us individually and collectively to commit to being the courageous voice that will always speak the Lord's truth, even when it is unpopular. Commit to tell those in power what the Lord has said. God's voice always calls to us to take up Christ's cross and standalone against the crowd.

Amen.

AM I DEALING WITH WHAT I AM FEELING?

By Sis. Jacqueline Norris

Many of us can say that initially dealing with COVID was rough but we made it. Some of us are still in the storm praying for it to end. The rest of us are looking into the tornado thinking Lord, why me? And asking God to let the damage bypass you.

For some of us the current environment, economic, and social justice issue is holding us back, restricting our happiness, stealing our joy, and causing much frustration.

What about you is allowing those situations to control you, your actions, and your behavior? The time has come, we need to determine, what we can do within the next 4 to 6 weeks to change our situation, to shift our perspective, to regain our joy and find strength to feel rejuvenated once again.

Today, I ask that where ever you are in your situation, take a moment to say thank you Lord. Thank him for the storm, thank him for the lesson, thank him for the people he sent you, thank him for the people he removed, and thank him for where he is taking you.

One area that might have a hold on us, showing up a negative impact, masking itself as something else and affecting our house of blessings is Life after Loss. You may be asking, why are we talking about this? Well, as Christians we tend to take on a lot and if we are not able to sort out our feelings it can have a negative impact on our worship experience and more so our service.

The statistics (100% fact or not) tell us that many people have contracted or have succumbed to the virus resulting in some type of loss. When we think of Loss, Loss of life comes quickly to our thoughts, probably because it can be one of the saddest flesh occasions or experiences, we have to face. Loss of life is definitely an area that none of us want to be an expert in. Today, I would also like to introduce a few other types of loss that may affect how we as Christian's worship and serve. These types of loss tend to have a huge impact on our faith but they are seldom properly addressed. Loss of relationships, jobs, opportunities, people, material items, support, money etc. COVID has taken many of these from us or for sure someone we know. While we know the Word instructs us not to place our hope in such things (Luke 12:15, 1 John 2:16-17, Ecclesiastes 5:10-11, Hebrews 13:5) we tend to "need" these to live comfortably on earth. So how do we handle Loss without becoming bitter and negative?

The good news is that we have the power to make a difference. We have the power to dictate our responses, our reactions, and our thinking. The power of influence is real and when you channel your energy you will find that you are your biggest source of influence. When loss occurs as a result of something that you cannot control (such as COVID), while you may feel a void, a hole, and an empty space the reality is that you still have an opportunity to exercise control.

Control of your behavior, thinking, and reaction. The pain of loss may never leave you and you may never fill that void but you have a choice to live, make decisions, and continue on your path. Life without your loved one will never be the same, and for some life without your stuff can be almost unbearable. However, the fact is, as long as you still have breath in your body you have the power to make it. As long as you continue to maintain a constant and healthy relationship with God you can be victorious.

This is not talking about your church relationship but about your TRUE connection with the Master! Call on Him and let Him deliver you so you can live free of guilt, shame, and worry.

Amen.

PRIORITIES

By Sis. Lecia Wilson

Make Time for Your Priorities. How do we put God first in our busy lives? Pray to God declaring that you want to open your life up to Him and invite Him to be more involved in your everyday life. Make a commitment to pray every morning and night, or before every meal.

God knows us better than we know ourselves. Since He is God our Creator, Sustainer, and Father, He knows what is best for our life now and our life to come. As we read through the written Word of God, we can see the priorities that God has established for our life. To prioritize means to arrange or complete a task in order of priority or rank. We need to recognize the priorities that God wants in our life.

When we seek Scriptural priorities, we discover those relationships, activities, and pursuits that should precede others in term of rank and order. God wants us to prioritize all of the possible activities in life according to these spiritual priorities.

What does God's Word say our priorities should be? The following scriptures can help us to establish the chief ones:

Matthew 6:33 But seek first the kingdom of God and His righteousness, and all these things shall be added to you.

Matthew 22:37-38 Jesus said to him, You shall love the Lord your God with all your heart, with all your soul, and with all your mind. This is the first and great commandment.

We need to be able to look at the alternatives and choose what is most pleasing to God and what is necessary for our spiritual wellbeing, and what would be a blessing to others. Once that has been established, we can better prioritize the numerous activities that compete for our attention.

Luke 12:34 For where your treasure is, there your heart will be also

Romans 12:1-2 I beseech you therefore, brethren, by the mercies of God, that you present your bodies a living sacrifice, holy, acceptable to God, which is your reasonable service. And do not be conformed to this world, but be transformed by the renewing of your mind, that you may prove what is that good and acceptable and perfect will of God.

Philippians 4:6-8 Be anxious for nothing, but in everything by prayer and supplication, with thanksgiving, let your requests be made known to God; and the peace of God, which surpasses all understanding, will guard your hearts and minds through Christ Jesus. Finally, brethren, whatever things are true, whatever things are noble, whatever things are just, whatever things are pure, whatever things are lovely, whatever things are of good report, if there is any virtue and if there is anything praiseworthy meditate on these things.

How do you put GOD at the center of your relationship?

Strengthen your personal relationship with God

Love God first before others

Fear the Lord

Pray for each other

Pray together

Study God's Word together

By doing this we will be putting Jesus Christ first in our life. If we exalt God above everyone and everything else, if we consistently seek first the kingdom of God, and if we strive for love and every other spiritual fruit, then our life will reveal this perspective. Our life will give clear evidence that our perspective on life is radically different from those around us. We will walk in Christ's -likeness according to God's Word. Surely, we will recognize God's written Word as a daily priority and we will devote ourselves to reading and studying its sacred contents to learn about God, His truth, and His will for our life.

Final Thought: Let us set our priorities straight, so that we can be sure we are putting God first always.

Amen.

A HEALING TOUCH

By Rev. Bobby Brown
Matthew 9:18-26

In today's lesson, two people are healed. Both experiences captured by the writer. Matthew shows that miracles are possible to those who dare to trust in the Lord. Regardless of your experience with your earthly father, everyone has the loving care of a heavenly father, who watches over all of his children. The Bible commands us to give honor to whom it is due (Romans 13:7) and to give particular honor to our father (Exodus 20:12). Our heavenly father blesses us by using the hands and hearts of those he brings into our lives. By faith reach for Jesus. Matthew 9:22 reads, "But Jesus turned him about and when he saw her he said, Daughter, be of good comfort; thy faith hath made thee whole. And the woman was made whole from that hour." Her simple yet bold act of faith led to her full deliverance. The woman was totally healed mind, body, and soul- and was able to return to her family and community to testify.

Miraculous healings happen all around us daily. Too often we fail to share our greatest spiritual experiences with others. Many believers have known God to be a healer or deliver. Yet, in times of crises, they can become so overwhelmed in the weight of the moment that they lose sight of the only one that can truly help them. Our challenge is to trust in God in every aspect of our lives.

To do anything other than trust in the Lord can cause us to miss out on life-changing blessings.

Pray for the guidance of the Holy Spirit to lead you and reveal the answer to your situation. Expect God to do what only he can. Rejoice in the healing power of God as manifested in your life.

Amen.

WHAT IS IN YOUR HEART
By Sis. Lecia Wilson

What does it mean as a man thinketh in his heart so is he? For as the thoughts of his heart are, so is he, means that a person's true nature is not always visible, sometimes they appear generous on the outside but they are really selfish or greedy on the inside. One of the most amazing gifts that God has given us is the human mind. The ability to learn, think, choose, and reason is the essence of what makes us human. While the ability to think makes us human, it's actually much deeper than that. Your thoughts become a reflection of who you really are. God certainly understands this, and he speaks to this in various places all throughout his Word. Proverbs 23:7, For as he thinks in his heart, so is he. Eat and drink! He says to you, But his heart is not with you. What you see in this verse is a person who is saying one thing with their mouth but their heart is in a completely different place.

When faced with this conundrum, which one do you believe? We tend to believe what is in the heart. The thoughts and inclinations of the heart shape the reality of who we are. They shape our thinking which will ultimately shape our actions. That is why what we think about matters, because it is forming the basis of who we will become. However, there is something about this verse that cannot be overlooked. Who you are on the inside and what you say on the outside, do not always line up.

God is concerned, primarily, about your heart. He wants you to have a healthy heart. 1 Samuel 16:7, But the Lord said to Samuel, Do not look at his appearance or at his physical stature, because I have refused him. For the Lord does not see as man sees; for man looks at the outward appearance, but the Lord looks at the heart.

His teaching goes back to the book of Proverbs where the writer emphasizes the importance of the heart. Lord, help me to take your words and bind them upon my heart. When I walk, may they guide me. When I sleep, may they watch over me. When I awake, may they speak to me. May they be like a lamp and a light keeping me on the way to life. Guard my heart, Lord.

Deuteronomy 10:16 Therefore circumcise the foreskin of your heart, and be stiff-necked no longer.

The Pharisees, for example, were very good at presenting themselves as very pious, devout, religious people, yet Jesus called them hypocrites. This word hypocrite in the Greek means actor. The Pharisees were playing a role on the outside that did not reflect who they really were. If you need to know who a person really is, you cannot always determine that by the things they say, you have to look at the root of who they are, and that root is the heart. (Ref Matthew 23:13-15 & Matthew 23:27-28). Woe to you, scribes and Pharisees, hypocrites! For you are like whitewashed tombs which indeed appear beautiful outwardly, but inside are full of dead men's bones and all uncleanness. Even so you also outwardly appear righteous to men, but inside you are full of hypocrisy and lawlessness.

Lord, forgive me for the times that I have been concerned about status or show. Help me to be myself and not try to pretend that I am anything better than I am. Help me to focus not on outward appearance but on the heart. Merciful Lord, you know our struggle to serve you: when sin spoils our lives and overshadows our hearts, come to our aid and return us back to you; through Jesus Christ our Lord.

Everything a person is flows out of their heart. Jesus said you will know a tree by its fruit. The core of who you are is evidenced by the thoughts or roots of your heart. That is why what is on the inside is so much more important than what is on the outside. You can mask the outside, and you can try to bury it to the world around you. Ultimately, what is in your heart will eventually reveal who you really are.

Amen.

BE AWARE OF ANGER & MALICE

By Sis. Jacqueline Norris
Ephesians 4:31

___

As we deal with open racism and prejudice behavior, we must continue to seek God, Trust God, and Believe that he has COMPLETE control. With that said, many Christians do not put much thought into anger and malice; yet as we move today, we are seeing it, feeling it, and trying to deal with it. Most feel that these two acts are done by people who are literally angry or people who commit horrible crimes. Many have turned a blind eye to the fact that anger and malice are real factors or issues for all humans and that it is possible for Christians to possess or commit either or both of these two root sins at any given time; especially when confronted with injustice based on something that we cannot control; our skin color. Christians need to be aware of and acknowledge what they are feeling and how it affects others, their faith, and their spiritual growth.

Anger is defined as a strong feeling of annoyance, displeasure, or hostility. Malice is defined as the intention or desire to do evil. When you put these two together, we have a big problem! If we are honest many of us are feeling, experienced, or have shared some or all of these emotions.

What does the Word say about these two things?

<u>Psalms 37:8</u> Refrain from anger, and forsake wrath! Fret not yourself; it tends only to evil.

Proverbs 15:18 A hot-tempered man stirs up strife, but he who is slow to anger quiets contention.

Proverbs 29:22 A man of wrath stirs up strife, and one given to anger causes much transgression.

Ecclesiastes 7:9 Be not quick in your spirit to become angry, for anger lodges in the bosom of fools

1 Peter 2:1-2 Therefore, putting aside all malice and all deceit and hypocrisy and envy and all slander, like newborn babies, long for the pure milk of the word, so that by it you may grow in respect to salvation,

Colossians 3:8 But now you also, put them all aside: anger, wrath, malice, slander, and abusive speech from your mouth

As I was researching the Scriptures, I found this version of Romans 1:28-32 and the message was received loud and clear for me many of the destruction that we are seeing is a result of disobedience, feeling of insecurity, or issues with control. The scripture reads, "People did not think it was important to have a true knowledge of God. So God left them and allowed them to have their own worthless thinking. And so they do what they should not do. They were filled with every kind of sin, evil, greed, and hatred. They were full of jealousy, murder, fighting, lying, and thinking the worst things about each other. They gossip and say evil things about each other. They hate God. They are rude, proud, and brag about themselves. They invent ways of doing evil. They don't obey their parents, they are foolish, they don't keep their promises, and they show no kindness or mercy to others. They know God's law says that anyone who lives like that should die. But they not only continue to do these things themselves, but they also encourage others who do them. (Basically, they teach this evil doing throughout the family).

Christians who find themselves out of touch with God find themselves on a dangerous road. Many have become so involved with self that they do not realize just how far they have strayed from God's will, His protection, His grace, His Love, and the damage being done to the relationship with Him. If we are not careful, Satin can grab a hold of us and slowly but surely what we once thought was sinful can begin to feel natural and lead us further and further away from the loving arms of God yet still claim a true commitment to GOD. With that said, malice and anger have the power to hinder spiritual growth and righteous living. It is difficult to reach out to God's children if you are angry, bitter, or holding grudges. If we are commissioned to worship on one accord, it will be difficult to worship the Lord in spirit and in truth if we are harvesting sin within our hearts. God calls us to be united, but if there is anger and malice present, we cannot do the work of the Lord and savior.

Amen.

EMPTY RITUALS ARE USELESS
By Rev. Bobby Brown
Isaiah 29:13-24

God's chosen people, the Nation of Israel, became guilty of allowing their worship to become nothing more than empty rituals. God used the prophet Isaiah to show them the uselessness of approaching him with insincerity while expecting to receive continued blessings. God is ever present and all-knowing. Nothing can ever be hidden for him- not our deeds, our thoughts, or the intentions of our hearts. True worship honors God by being God-centered rather than self-centered. Self-centered worship treats God as the created and not the creator.

The purpose of discipline is restoration rather than condemnation. God disciplines his children to bring about spiritual transformation in their lives in preparation for promised blessings. When their worship is genuine, true believers can trust God to forgive and restore in spite of great personal failure. Worship that is sincere and God-focused transforms the worshipper in the presence of God. Worship focused on personal gratification rather than giving God the glory and honor he deserves is simply a meaningless ritual with no possibility of spiritual transformation.

God is not moved by empty religious rituals that have no regard for God's presence and fail to glorify him for who he is. Judah's spiritual condition deteriorated to the point that their worship was nothing more than lip service. In their minds, God's own people elevated themselves above God. They depended on their own intellect for deliverance rather than trusting God to provide. Believers who turn their focus away from God become guilty of giving lip-service to God. Distracted, superficial worship that is merely a matter of habit and obligation means nothing to God.

Amen.

ARE YOU COMFORTABLE IN SIN?

By Sis. LaTasha Marie Knighten

One of the biggest mistakes we make as Christians today is that we are comfortable with sitting in our sin or ok with watching other people sin and decide to be silent about it. We know right from wrong but we often turn the other cheek or cover our eyes just so we can make other people feel comfortable for the moment.

When we become comfortable with our sin it simply shows that we are spiritually immature and that we need to seek God for help and for guidance. Often Christians tend to make a big deal about the following sins: fortification, adultery, stealing or lying. Somehow most of us tend to leave out cheating, hoarding, overeating, being manipulative, and the main one lack of trust when it comes to God's word. Please know that sin is sin and no matter how we try when we go against God's word we are sinning. God gives us free will and it is up to us to resist temptation and follow God's way.

We also must remember to be careful of how we talk to others as we try to redirect them from sin. The best way to redirect others is to show them God's word, so they can see it for themselves. Romans 3:23 tells us we have all sinned and come short of the glory of God and 2 Timothy 3:16 reminds us that all Scripture is God-breathed and is useful for teaching, rebuking, correcting and training in righteousness,

The key phrase is that we all have sinned and we have no business casting stones. Casting stones simply means applying judgement on one another. We should make it our business to share His word and extend love as well as giving mutual respect instead of casting stones.

Always remember that no matter what we are going through or facing God is always with us and we must not forget God. Some of us leave Him in our purse our backpacks. After the church service we leave Him in our cars and some never take Him out of the church. The whole time God is saying, "Hey, I'm here. Come seek me and I will give you life".

Here are some tips to ensure that you are not comfortable in Sin:

1. Stay connect to God.//
2. Make sure your relationship with God is the priority. For this to be so important you might be surprised to know that it is not hard.
3. Don't get consumed by what you are going through in your daily life. We must make sure that God is the center of our lives.
4. Remember that He is the supplier of all our needs.

When I say make your relationship with God a priority you must first acknowledge Him and second ask for direction. That is hard for some of us because we already have our minds set before we even begin our day. We make our own plans but fail to ask God what we should and should not be doing. In these situations, repentance is key. Ask God to forgive you for making plans without consulting him.

What we want and what God wants for us do not always line up. There is difference between our needs and our wants. God's peace or pleasure is not the same as our earthly peace or pleasure. We must realize that our current self-care routines result in momentary peace or pleasure but the peace that we should be trying to achieve is God's peace.

We can achieve that peace by realizing, knowing, and trusting that God is in control. In doing so that calls for us to trust God to handle the difficult situations that occur in life and understanding that vengeance belongs to the Lord not us.

My sisters and brothers hide His word in your heart and seek Him for he is the giver of purpose and wisdom. Never be comfortable in sin even if it feels good for the moment.

Never give up on God because God will never give up on you!

Amen.

DO YOU HAVE A RELATIONSHIP WITH GOD?

By Rev. Jackey Wilson

What is a relationship? It is the manner in which two people or two groups behave or relate towards each other.

In today's world a professional relationship should not be affected by personal feelings because feelings can cause problems in a situation. A relationship between a mother and daughter, a father and son, or a husband and wife is based on love and feelings toward each other.

But my question is, "How is your relationship with God"? Is your relationship with God professional or personal? Do you merely associate with Him or do you know and love Him? God relates to us on a personal level. He truly knows and loves us. Evidence of this can be found in John 3:16: "For God so loved the world he gave his only begotten son." Genesis 1:27: "God created us in his image." And lastly, "God sent his son not to condemn us but to save the world." (John 3:17.) We need to get to know God better. Not based upon someone else's account, but get to know Him for ourselves. We need to know that He is our way out of any situation or temptation. (1st Corinthians 10:13). Whenever we are in need, we can call upon Him. Yet, in order for this to be affective there are two things you must do:

1) Believe in your Heart;

2) Confess with your mouth that Jesus Died and the Father rose Him up with all power.

Once this is completed, you are saved. When you are saved your faith will increase and you will be able to witness first hand, that God will do just what He said. So, seek, find and have a relationship with God.

Amen.

CONCLUSION

As a Sunday School Teacher I encourage you today to remove negative thoughts or anything that is controlling your mind and behavior. Start by recognizing who God created you to be, constantly pray for change, teach those who yearn to be taught, be a role model for those who look to you for guidance, love those who hate the Word, live your life based on the principals noted in the Bible, and last but not least stand on the fact that God is in control. Know that there is no reason to fear or have doubt – He will provide, empower, and equip you for servitude!

In times like these, draw on your inner power, pour into yourself, indulge in self-love, make time for time, and make taking care of you a priority. (Yes, I am talking to me too). This is not selfish; it is a tool that you can use to refresh and recharge so that you can please God and live free!

"Finally, brethren, whatever things are true, whatever things are noble, whatever things are just, whatever things are pure, whatever things are lovely, whatever things are of good report, if there is any virtue and if there is anything praiseworthy — meditate on these things." Philippians 4:8

"And we know that in all things God works for the good of those who love him, who have been called according to his purpose." Romans 8:28

EVERGREEN BAPTIST CHURCH HISTORY

Rev. Ruth Johnson stated that God lead him to go to San Francisco to build a church between two mountains. Thus the Evergreen Baptist Church was founded in 1945.

It started with just Sunday school, which was held in his home at 2501 Ingalls in South Basin. He had approximately 26 people, of which included five to six families, the Pryor's, the Williams, the Jackson's, the Waller's, the Fords, and Sis. Green, who served as the first secretary of the church.

In 1946, Pastor Johnson found a store front building located at 6270 Third Street in San Francisco and that was the beginning of the Evergreen Missionary Baptist Church. This is the current location, although the seating was facing towards the mountain.

Pastor Johnson served the church with a God-fearing attitude, which challenged his parishioners to focus on having a Christ like attitude. He organized and was the overseer of all auxiliaries. Many pastors, ministers, and teachers have come through Evergreen and several Bay Area Churches were formed under the leadership of Pastor Johnson. Pastor Johnson served the Evergreen Baptist church faithfully until his health failed in June of 1991.

In 1991, the church elected Rev. Christopher Jones. As God would have it, Rev. Johnson felt well enough to preach his installation message and give him the charge. Rev. Jones served the church until he resigned in March of 1995.

In 1995, Rev. James Greenwood was called as the Pastor. He served the church faithfully for more than 5 years and under his leadership the Ruth Circle was re-organized, the Vacation Bible School and the Youth Revival was organized, and through God's guidance the Church was blessed with the opportunity to purchase the property next door to the church. Due to his mother's health Pastor Greenwood resigned and relocated to San Antonio Texas in 2002.

After the resignation of Pastor Greenwood, Minister Dexter Landers carried on the ministerial duties of the church serving as Interim Pastor. This was a very vital role, his dedication & willingness to serve was valued and much appreciated.

In February 2003, the Evergreen Church welcomed Rev. Damien Epps to be the Pastor and Shepherd. During Pastor Epps' 5-year tenure and leadership the church experienced tremendous change and abundant spiritual growth. Pastor Epps presented the church with his resignation in July of 2008.

In August of 2008, Reverend Jackey J. Wilson Sr. was asked to carry on the ministerial duties of the church and to serve as the Interim Pastor. In October of 2008, the members of the Evergreen Baptist Church voted to accept Rev. Wilson as the Pastor and he readily accepted the assignment. Under Pastor Wilson's leadership Evergreen has witnessed the spiritual growth of the Higher Praise dance ministry, the Jr. Praise dance ministry was formed, the construction at the property located at 6276 Third Street was completed, central air and heating was installed within the sanctuary, the sanctuary restrooms were remodeled, a Thursday Night Bible Study in East Palo Alto was added, new chairs and curtains were purchased for the Social Hall. In 2009 Reverend Bobbie Brown accepted his calling to preach. On October 2, 2015 Deacons Richard Norris and Quincy Danastorg were ordained. In October of 2017 the following upgrades were made to the Social Hall: replacement of the main entryway front doors, the front stair case was re-cemented & painted, the back stairs were reinforced, and the building received a fresh coat of paint. Also, in 2017 the EBC food pantry was reinstituted and two new ministries were added for sharing with the homeless; along with the Norris Family feeding the needy the We Care Ministry distributes blankets, socks, and hygiene packs. In 2018 security doors were added to the church building and a noon day bible study was added. In 2019 Minister Deandre Lathan accepted his calling to preach and preached his first sermon on May 19th 2019 and on February 22, 2020 he was ordained.

On March 15, 2020 as a result of the COVID-19 virus many Bay Area churches including Evergreen Baptist Church, under the direction of Mayor London Breed, were instructed to close the physical doors of the church and members directed to Shelter in Place. By the grace of God, that did not stop the members of Evergreen from extending worship and Praise to Our Lord and Savior. Thanks to Sister Jacque Norris, on March 18, 2020 our first virtual ministry was established, a Monday thru Saturday noon day Prayer Line. On March 28, 2020 our first virtual Sunday school was instituted and taught by Sis. Jacqueline Norris and facilitated by Sis. Latasha Knighten. On March 31, 2020 our first virtual Wednesday night Bible Study was instituted and taught by First Lady Lecia Wilson. On April 5, 2020 our members experienced the 1st virtual Communion service facilitated by Rev. Kevin Barbour from Texas, over 30 communion packages were delivered to member's homes prior to Sunday morning Service. On April 20, 2020 a weekly Thursday program hosted & facilitated by JN Outreach titled Let's Talk was introduced to Evergreen. On April 26, 2020 a full morning service was added to the Sunday morning service (to include a sermon from Pastor Wilson as well as a song from Sis. Stephanie Williams-Andrew). On May 22, 2020 Deacon Richard Norris hosted a Senior Social where 28 dinners were distributed to the Seniors of Evergreen by Deacon and Sis. Norris, Pastor, First Lady Wilson, and Sis. Alicia Ward. On July 2, 2020 Pastor Wilson instituted an opening on the Prayer Line for the children and youth to pray and talk to God. On July 8, 2020 a virtual 10-minute Monday through Friday live Devotional Reading commenced. On August 1, 2020 First Lady Wilson initiated a mobile prayer box service. This allows the members to write their prayers and place them into a secure prayer box when they receive their in-person Communion deliveries. On August 11, 2020 Pastor Wilson along with Sis. LaTasha Knighten conducted the 1st virtual one hour Youth Meeting on Tuesday evenings. On August 7, 2020 Pastor Wilson added virtual Friday Night Service where the preachers of Evergreen present the Word starting at 6PM. COVID-19 has presented many challenges for the community, churches, and families but we are proud to say that thus far, we have successfully connected with people from the following areas: SF, San Jose, Los Angeles, Sacramento, Stockton, Menlo Park, Palo

Alto, Roseville, Vacaville, and Brentwood in addition to the following States: Michigan, Minnesota, Texas, Indiana, and Ohio.

In 2021 Evergreen Baptist Church celebrated its 76th Anniversary. We are proud to say that we are still going strong and reaching lives in surrounding communities. We have conducted Church services over the phone for over two years and God has continued to bless us each Sunday Morning with an average of 35 to 40 callers. God is still in the blessing business.

As evident above, the Evergreen Family is committed to continuously maintaining and moving our spiritual lives forward according to God's Word and direction.

While we continue to be an active part of our community, we ask that each member and friend of Evergreen continue to pray and have an unmovable faith. God has truly blessed the Evergreen Baptist Church not just on Sunday Morning but 7 days a week 24/7 since 1945!

You can join our services On Sunday Morning at 10:45AM by calling 1-712-832-8559 or 1-712-832-8330 and enter access code 2703554.

SPECIAL THANKS

I would like to extend my sincere appreciation to Rev. Bobby Brown, Rev. Abraham Gunter, First Lady Lecia Wilson, Sis. Latasha Knighten, and Pastor Jackey Wilson for their submissions to this book.

Thank you for trusting me with your words and allowing this book to represent what we all believe in, a strong FOUNDATION IN our Lord and Savior. Thank you for allowing me to share your heartfelt messages with the intent to Make a Difference and Impact Lives all over the world!

Jaaz Nspiration Publications

Impacting Lives and Making a Difference (2018)

My Prayer Have the Power to Make a Difference (2019)

Rejuvenation of Mind Body and Soul for Teens (2020)

On Sunday Morning, The Collection (2021)

Publications can be purchased from Amazon, by visiting WWW.JAAZWORLD.COM/SHOP, or by calling 415-596-6595.

Can You Find 16 Bible Books
In The Paragraph Below?

I once made some remarks about hidden books in the bible. It was a lulu; kept some people looking so hard for facts, and to others it was a revelation. Some were in a jam, especially since the books were not capitalized. But the truth finally struck home to numbers of readers. To others it was a really job. We want it to be a most fascinating few minutes for you.

Yes, there will be some really easy ones to spot. Others might require judges to determine. We will quickly admit it usually takes a minister to find one, and there will be loud lamentations when you see how easy it is. A little lady says that if she brews tea she can concentrate better. See how well you compete. Relax, now, there are 16 in this paragraph.

Mark, Luke, Kings, Acts, Revelation, James, Ruth, Numbers, Job, Amos, Esther, Judges, Titus, Lamentations, Hebrews, Peter

AUTHOR BIO

Jacqueline Marie Sanders-Norris "Jacque"

Summary

Born and raised in San Francisco, Human Resources Professional, Entrepreneur, Author, Crafter, Inspirational Speaker, Teacher/Educator, Wife, Mother of five, Grandmother of four, Cancer survivor, and Christian.

Professional Experience

Has been in the Human Resource field for 30+ years. Employed by City and County of San Francisco as a Human Resource Analyst since 2006. Owner of Jaaz Creative Designs featuring handcrafted greeting cards and jewelry established in 2015. Author of Jaaz Nspirations providing consistent positive affirmations via technology, website published in 2016. Author of Impacting Lives and Making a Difference (2018), My Prayers Have the Power to Make a Difference (2019), Rejuvenation of Mind, Body, and Soul for Teens (2020), and On Sunday Morning (2021). Founder and Executive Director of JN Outreach Foundation, Inc. (501c3) officially incorporated in 2018. Owner of JN Notary & Professional Services (2021).

Education Summary

Graduated from Immaculate Conception Academy in 1989 (GPA 3.85), PHR certified in 2003, received AA Degree in Communication in 2011 (GPA 3.70), BS Degree in Management in

2014 (GPA 3.65), and Masters in Adult Education in 2016 (GPA 3.91).

Spiritual Leadership

Currently resides in San Francisco, CA where she has been a member of the Evergreen Baptist Church (50 yrs), Member (22 yrs)/President of the Usher Board (9 yrs), Member of the Deaconess Board (6 yrs), Finance Clerk (15 yrs), Previous Young Adult Sunday School Teacher (5 yrs), Current Adult Sunday School teacher (14 yrs), Inspirational Leader (3yrs), and a Member (6 yrs)/ Teacher (2 yr) of the Deaconess Auxiliary Board at the St. John District Congress of Christian Education.

Notes

www.ingramcontent.com/pod-product-compliance
Lightning Source LLC
LaVergne TN
LVHW051202080426
835508LV00021B/2757